MOIN and the MONKEY MONSTER

Read more about MOIN

Moin and the Monster
Moin the Monster Songster

Read the SMARTYPANTS series

Evolution for Smartypants
Gravity for Smartypants
Rocket Science for Smartypants
Cell Theory for Smartypants
Newton's Laws of Motion for Smartypants
Earthquakes for Smartypants
Vaccines for Smartypants
Set Theory for Smartypants
Photosynthesis for Smartypants

Scan QR code to access the
Penguin Random House India website

MOIN and THE MONKEY MONSTER

Anushka Ravishankar

Illustrations by
Anitha Balachandran

An imprint of Penguin Random House

To all those who wanted Moin 3—Merry Christmas!

DUCKBILL BOOKS

Duckbill Books is an imprint of the Penguin Random House group of companies whose addresses can be found at global.penguinrandomhouse.com

Published by Penguin Random House India Pvt. Ltd
4th Floor, Capital Tower 1, MG Road,
Gurugram 122 002, Haryana, India

 Penguin
Random House
India

First published in Duckbill Books by Penguin Random House India 2025

Text copyright © Anushka Ravishankar 2025
Illustrations copyright © Anitha Balachandran 2025

Anushka Ravishankar asserts the moral right to be identified as the author of this work.

All rights reserved

10 9 8 7 6 5 4 3 2 1

This is a work of fiction. Names, characters, places and incidents are either the product of the author's imagination or are used fictitiously and any resemblance to any actual person, living or dead, events or locales is entirely coincidental.

Please note that no part of this book may be used or reproduced in any manner for the purpose of training artificial intelligence technologies or systems.

ISBN 9780143478300

Typeset in Weiss by DiTech Publishing Services Pvt. Ltd
Printed at Acme Print O Pac Pvt. Ltd . Noida

This book is sold subject to the condition that it shall not, by way of trade or otherwise, be lent, resold, hired out, or otherwise circulated without the publisher's prior consent in any form of binding or cover other than that in which it is published and without a similar condition including this condition being imposed on the subsequent purchaser.

www.penguin.co.in

PREVIOUSLY...
HOW MOIN GOT A MONSTER

One night, in the dim darkness of his room, Moin heard something shuffling and sniffling under his bed.

It was a monster, but Moin could not see it until he drew it. So the monster described itself, and Moin drew it.

The monster was most displeased. 'I'm supposed to be fearsome!' it complained. 'You've made me look funny.'

Moin was very annoyed at having his drawing criticized. 'I didn't ask you to hide under my bed and wake me up in the middle of the night,' he sulked.

But Moin and the monster were stuck together because of the monster rules.

And it looked like they would have to stay together forever.

*Eyes like flames
And nose like pails
Ears like horns
And teeth like nails
A scary, fearsome sight to see
Monster, monster, monster me!*

*Skull-shaped mole
On rock-like chin
Long green hair
And purple skin
In the dark you'll scream to see
Monster, monster, monster ME!*

*Drum-shaped chest
And arms like trees
Bamboo legs on
Feet like skis
Terrifying as can be
Monster, monster, monster
MEEEEEEEEEE!*

PREVIOUSLY...
HOW MOIN LOST A MONSTER

It was all the monster's fault.

Loopy Bagiri loved the monster's voice, though, of course, he thought it was Moin's.

But the monster refused to sing Loopy's song, So Moin had to sing instead. Loopy felt Moin's voice was too sweet and sent a potion for Moin.

But the monster drank it and disappeared.

MONSTER RULE 321

Human products can have unpredictable side effects on monsters.

Bananas, Bananas

The bananas were the problem.

It was almost two weeks since the monster had disappeared, and things had changed a lot.

Moin was happy that he didn't have to hear the monster's horrible songs. They made his ears hurt.

And he didn't have to keep cleaning the mess in his room.

He also didn't have to pretend to sing so that his parents wouldn't realize that it was the monster shrieking.

All that was good.

But the bananas made Moin sick. Ever since the monster had turned up, Moin had taken great pains to pretend that he loved bananas. He didn't dislike them—he could eat two a day, maybe three at a pinch. But the monster's demands for bananas were never-ending, so Moin had had to pretend he wanted to eat them all the time.

Now his parents kept buying bananas and telling him to finish them before they got spoilt. He'd taken to hiding them in his bag and chucking them in the bin at school. But all his books had begun to smell like rotten bananas.

Moin's maths teacher had refused to mark his last test, saying the smell made her retch. And he had been so sure he'd get full marks.

So, he had to stop the bananas.

But how?

If he said his stomach was upset, his mother would rush him to the bald doctor. Moin was convinced the doctor hated him. It could be because of the spit bubble he had burst the last time he had visited the doctor, or it could just be that he hated children. Moin strongly suspected that he had become a paediatrician just to torture small children and make them cry.

If he said he had stopped liking bananas, he would get a lecture on children in some country called Somasila. No wait, that was a village in Andhra Pradesh. Or maybe Telangana. If they kept changing states so rapidly, how was he to keep up?

Somalia! That's the country he would be lectured about. What the children in Somasila or Somalia had to do with him liking food was something that puzzled Moin endlessly. But if he ever said 'I don't like karela' or 'I don't like beetroot', he'd get an earful about starving children in different parts of the world.

'We can't send the karela to them, so how does it matter?' he had asked once.

He was made to eat karela for a week after that. It wasn't that his parents were cruel or anything. Actually, he suspected that his father had bought too much karela at the market. The seller must have told him a sad story of some sort. But his father pretended that it was a punishment for Moin. Convenient! Moin was beginning to see through his parents' devious methods.

'The only way the bananas will stop is if they are replaced by something else,' Moin said to his friends at school the next day, having given the matter a lot of thought.

'Chocolates?' asked his best friend Tony, always optimistic.

'Huh. That'll never work,' said Parvati, his other best friend. 'They'll never buy dozens of chocolates. It'll have to be a fruit or a vegetable.'

'It has to be something I like,' said Moin, 'because I'll have to eat a lot of it.'

'I know what!' said Parvati. 'Ask for something really expensive. Then they can't get you too much of it.'

'Or seasonal,' said Tony. 'Like mangosteen! That's costly *and* seasonal.'

Moin had never heard of a mangosteen. He guessed it was something like a mango. He loved mangoes!

So that evening, he told his father, 'I wish I could eat some mangosteen.'

'It's out of season. Have a banana,' said Mr Kaif.

Moin went to his room, muttering about stupid banana-eating monsters and insensitive fathers.

The next morning there were more bananas on the table. Moin ate his breakfast quickly.

'I got you some more bananas,' his mother said.

Moin groaned.

'What is it?' his mother asked anxiously. 'Does your stomach hurt? Does your head ache?'

'I don't want any more bananas,' Moin said grumpily. 'I'm sick of them. I don't care if I never see another banana in my life.'

'Oh god, we're going to get banana pulao again!' groaned Mrs Kaif.

The last time they had a lot of uneaten bananas in the house, Mr Kaif had scoured the internet for recipes and made all sorts of banana things. Moin and his mother agreed that the banana pulao was the worst of the lot.

While Mr Kaif had eaten it valiantly, Mrs Kaif and Moin had nibbled at it. They would have picked out the bananas, but the rice was banana-flavoured too!

Late that night, when Mr Kaif had been sleeping, Mrs Kaif had thrown away the rest of the pulao, and Moin and she had eaten a whole loaf of bread with butter.

Moin shuddered at the memory.

'We *have* to get rid of the bananas,' he said to his mother.

Unfortunately, Mr Kaif walked in at that moment.

'What about the bananas? If you don't want to eat them, I have this really interesting recipe that—'

'No, no!' said Mrs Kaif, immediately.

'I'll eat them!' said Moin, just as quickly.

He took the bananas to his room. He had to figure out a way to get rid of them, but he was late for school, so he shoved them under his bed and left.

That evening, when he came back, Moin got a terrible shock.

The bananas were gone.

THE SCIENTIFIC TEMPERAMENT

'I think it's back!' Moin croaked.

'Why do you sound like you've eaten a frog?' asked Parvati.

Moin and Tony were at Parvati's house to spend the day.

Moin took a deep breath and tried again. 'I think the monster is back.'

'Yay!' shouted Tony. He was the only one who was truly sad that the monster had gone.

Parvati had said, 'Thank goodness I don't have to listen to that horrible singing again.'

Moin had said nothing. He'd always had a niggling feeling the monster would be back.

And now he was proved right. How else could the bananas have disappeared?

'Bah. Anything could have happened. Maybe your mother threw them away. Maybe your father made a giant banana milkshake and drank it up. Maybe rats ate them. Maybe a monkey got into your room and ran off with them. The monster has gone away,' Parvati declared.

'It couldn't have gone away. It had to stay here forever,' said Moin.

'Yes,' said Tony. 'That was monster rule number 54. The monster did tell me that I should also see rules 71, 228 and 364. But it couldn't remember what they were.'

They sat in silence and wondered once again where the monster could be.

They had discussed this ad nauseam the weekend after the monster had dramatically vanished.

Ad nauseam, as Tony had explained, meant 'until one got tired of it'. Parvati didn't think that was right. She felt it meant 'until one felt like puking'. They had argued about *that* ad nauseam, until Moin actually felt like puking. He wanted to agree with Parvati, but he didn't want to upset Tony, so he had quietly gone to the toilet and puked. It might have been because of the argument, but it might have also been because of the bananas.

No one wanted to start talking about it again, really, but they couldn't understand it at all.

'We should talk to a scientist,' said Parvati.

'Harimama?' asked Moin, doubtfully.

Harimama was Parvati's uncle. The last time they had seen him, he had been hugging his broken telescope and crying like a baby. Moin's stomach gave a little twinge at the thought. He was sure it was guilt, because he had not eaten any bananas.

'He's okay now. He's got a new telescope, and he was lecturing me about the wonders of science and something called the scientific temperament last week. I'll make up a story about a science project, and we can go and pick his brains.'

'What's a scientific temperament?' asked Moin, imagining Einstein throwing a tantrum.

'I have no idea,' Parvati shrugged. 'I can't pay attention to everything adults say, can I?'

Moin agreed, but Tony, of course, knew what a scientific temperament was. 'If you're always asking questions and trying to understand what's going on using science, instead of guesswork or superstition, it means you have a scientific temperament.'

'I don't have it, then. I'm very good at guessing things,' Moin said. He conveniently forgot how he had guessed a ski was like a broom. The monster would never forgive him for giving it feet that looked like brooms instead of skis.

'Whatever,' said Parvati, equally unimpressed with the scientific temperament and with Moin's guessing skills. 'Let's go see Harimama anyway. He's the only scientist we know.'

Harimama was free that afternoon, so Parvati's father dropped them off. Parvati's father liked to sound the horn when he was in the car. He also shouted at people on the road.

'Have you told them at home?' he'd shout to someone who turned without showing a signal. Parvati explained that it was a translation from Tamil, but she wasn't sure what it meant.

Or to someone who cut into his lane: 'Are those eyes or pajamas?'

Or to someone driving with a mobile phone to their ear: 'Are you letting them know you're about to kill people?'

He beeped loudly at anyone who came in the way and did a little happy rhythm of beeps when the road was empty and the driving was smooth. It was all very entertaining but also very stressful.

By the time they tumbled out of the car, all three of them were half deaf and totally terrified. Actually, just two of them. Parvati was used to it and was grinning happily.

'Don't touch that telescope, okay?' her father warned, as he left with a loud, long beep.

INVISIBILITY

Harimama was waiting for them with Small, his dog.

'Ha ha ha! Here come the scientists!' he guffawed, glancing back to make sure he had locked up his precious telescope.

Small sniffed at them and then jumped on them, so the next few minutes were a tangle of arms and legs and a cacophony of shrieks and giggles.

'So what is this science project?' asked Harimama, as they all lay on the ground, out of breath. 'Are you researching gravity? Ha ha!'

The children got up and sat on various chairs. They had made an elaborate plan about the science project, but now that they were here, the story seemed a bit thin.

'Er . . .' started Moin.

'Um . . .' said Tony.

'Can we have some lemonade, Harimama?' asked Parvati, looking daggers at her two gurgling friends.

When Harimama left the room, she turned to them, scowling. 'Er? Um? What happened to our plan? I told you we should have written it out.'

'He's not going to believe we are researching invisibility,' said Tony. Even his famed optimism could not overcome the ridiculousness of the plan.

'That sounds totally unscientific. He'll laugh at us.'

Parvati waved away their objections. 'Harimama is always laughing anyway. And invisibility *is* scientific. Harimama once told me about this book where a scientist uses optics to make himself invisible.'

'Optics? We can't use optics! That's illegal,' said Moin.

'Optics means the study of how light behaves,' explained Tony the encyclopedia.

'Exactly! So it's totally scientific! And anyway, we're only trying to figure out where the monster could have gone. We're not making ourselves invisible!'

'Invisible? Who is invisible?' asked Harimama, as he came in with four huge glasses of lemonade.

'No one is invisible, Harimama,' said Parvati. 'We want to learn about invisibility.'

'Hmm. I'm not sure your parents would approve of this line of inquiry. Why do you want to disappear? Have you been up to some mischief?'

'It's for a science project,' said Moin, putting on his best innocent look.

'How can people become invisible?' asked Parvati, coming straight to the point.

'That science has not been discovered yet.'

'But remember you told me about that book, by someone called Ponds or something?'

'Ponds? Like the people who make face powder and creams?'

'Ayyo, Harimama, no! Ponds, like with water. Or wait, maybe it was Canals. Remember that book about a man who becomes invisible?'

Harimama suddenly went red. Moin was alarmed. Last time, they had made him cry. This time, was he going to have a heart attack or something? Was he going to burst like a balloon?

'HA HA HA HA!' Harimama exploded. 'Canals? Ponds? Ha ha! Ha ha ha!'

Parvati was watching her uncle with a scowl. 'What's so funny?' she grumbled.

'Canals!' wept Harimama, hiccuping and laughing and crying, all at the same time.

Tony and Moin were grinning too. Not because they had any idea what Harimama was laughing about, but just because he looked so funny. His nose was red, his tummy was wobbling and, to make things funnier, Small was so excited to see Harimama laugh that he kept running around him in circles.

Finally, Harimama stopped laughing and wheezed for a minute or two. 'You . . . mean . . . Wells,' he panted, and started giggling again. Fortunately, he stopped quickly. 'H.G. Wells wrote a book called *The Invisible Man*. That was fiction, though.'

'Still, it was *science* fiction, right? So it was scientific?'

'The invisible man had figured out how to change his refractive index so that he would have the same refractive index as air, which means he would be invisible.'

Harimama beamed at three blank faces. He sometimes forgot that most nine-year-olds did not know words like refractive or index.

'Oh,' he said, registering how blank they looked. He thought for a moment. 'He figured out how to make himself look like air, so he wouldn't be visible. It's an ingenious idea, but it's not really possible.'

'But suppose it is,' said Moin, remembering how the monster had seemed to fade into the air. 'Maybe there's some special potion that makes your refrac-whatever thingy like air.'

'Yes, maybe you can drink it and become invisible?' asked Tony, who had immediately understood what Moin was thinking about.

'But can your voice become invisible too?' asked Moin.

'And what happens when you eat?' asked Parvati. 'If the food can be seen, can we see the food going into the invisible man without seeing the invisible man?'

'Yes, going into his mouth and getting all chewed up, then going down, down to his stomach and getting digested!' Moin's eyes grew round at the thought.

'Ewwww!' chorused Parvati and Tony.

'And what happens when he changes clothes? Will we be able to see the clothes without seeing the head and hands and feet of the person wearing the clothes?' Tony was clearly fascinated by this notion.

'Stop! Stop!' yelled Harimama, pretending to fend off an attack. He made them sit down and lectured them for an hour on optics. He used words like refractive index and optical illusion, and soon Moin began to understand why the monster used to start snoring as soon as it heard big words.

Then Harimama started off on sound and the frequencies that are not audible to the human ear.

Tony was taking notes. Moin was wondering if it would be too obvious if he used his fingers to keep his eyes open. Parvati was listening but was restless—she had decided this was all pointless. It was clear that none of this would

help them find out if the monster was coming back.

Small was sleeping soundly, to Moin's deep envy. He wished he were a dog. Being a human was hard work.

'So,' said Harimama, 'it is impossible to be invisible and inaudible given the development of science and technology today. Maybe some day in the future . . .'

'Eureka!' Tony yelled.

Moin, half asleep, woke up with a start. Small bounded up and jumped on Parvati's chair, knocking her off it.

'What?' she asked irritably as Moin and Tony helped her up.

'The future! Time travel!' said Tony, in such a loud stage whisper that Harimama couldn't help but hear.

'Aha!' he cried. 'Let's talk about time travel!'

'Er, we have to go,' said Parvati.

'YES!' shouted Moin. Then he realized he had said that too loudly, and whispered, 'Yes.'

Tony was the only one who showed any inclination to stay, but, luckily for the others, Parvati's father came to pick them up.

Fancy Dress

'What was that about?' Parvati asked Tony when they reached her house. They hadn't been able to speak in the car because of the horn blasts.

'I had a brilliant, brilliant thought. Remember how we thought the monster might have come from some other planet? What if it didn't come from another planet, but from another time!'

There was a stupefied silence. Then Moin and Parvati laughed and laughed. They laughed until their stomachs ached. Tony watched them, looking sad and hurt. But he waited patiently until they stopped laughing.

'It's totally possible. So maybe far, far in the future some new species will have evolved, and the monster belongs to that species. I mean, think about it. If there could be dinosaurs in the past, why can't there be monsters in the future?'

'That doesn't explain how it appeared when Moin drew it, or why it vanished after drinking that thing that Loopy sent for Moin.'

When Parvati mentioned Loopy, Moin's heart did a somersault. He suddenly remembered that he was supposed to sing at Loopy Bagiri's concert in two days. He really, really did not want to do it. But Loopy had already done so much publicity for the concert that Moin didn't have a choice. Neither did Loopy, actually.

Loopy was very unhappy with Moin's voice. When he had asked Moin to sing at his concert, it was because the monster had been singing from Moin's pocket. Loopy *loved* that voice, which he thought was Moin's. But now, the monster was gone and Loopy was bewildered, because Moin's voice had suddenly become too sweet. He didn't like it at all.

But the posters were up all over the city, the venue had been booked, and tickets had been sold.

'Argh! I'll have to sing at the concert!' groaned Moin.

'Erm, I think I might have violin class that day.'

'It's my grandfather's birthday . . .' Tony began, but he remembered that Parvati and Moin had come to celebrate his grandfather's birthday just last week.

Moin wished he could have some unmissable class that day. He was not looking forward to the concert. He found Loopy Bagiri's music unbearable. Worse still, Loopy's perfume made him feel like he was drowning in the armpit of some creature that had not had a bath since the beginning of time.

'Maybe I should ask him for more of that potion which he gave me. The monster finished it off. If I have some of it, maybe I'll go off to the distant future and won't have to do the concert,' said Moin thoughtfully.

The mystery of the bananas was solved when Moin got home. There were banana fritters for dessert.

'I found a whole bunch in your room when I went to clean up yesterday,' said Mr Kaif, 'so I decided to try this recipe.'

Thankfully, the fritters were quite tasty.

'After dinner, try out your costume,' said Mrs Kaif reminded Moin.

'Costume? What costume? I'm not taking part in a fancy-dress thingy!' said Moin, alarmed. He hated fancy-dress costumes.

They always reminded him of the time he had gone on stage dressed as Neil Armstrong. He was supposed to stand triumphantly on the moon (stage) and say 'One small step for man, one giant leap for mankind.'

But he had been so nervous, he froze. From the wings, his father hissed the words at him helpfully. But finally, the audience had started clapping, and his mother, laughing helplessly, had come on stage and carried him away. He had been only three and a half years old. And though he had overcome his fear of audiences since then, he'd never participated in a fancy-dress competition again.

'It's not a fancy-dress costume. It's for your show with Loopy.'

'I'd call it a fancy-dress costume,' muttered Mr Kaif. Mrs Kaif gave him a look.

When Moin saw his costume, he began to cough. That was because he'd started laughing first, but when it struck him that he would actually have to wear the costume, he began to hiccup with stress, and his breath caught in his throat.

By the time his mother hit him on the back (too hard, he felt), and his father made him drink a glass of water, his stress had turned to cold fear. He would have to wear *this* on stage?

'We know, it's a bit much,' his mother said kindly.

'It's just one song. Sing it and leave.'

'But the whole crowd will watch. And there'll be videos and everything! I can't wear this,' said Moin, his voice squeaky with indignation. 'We'll tell him it doesn't fit. We'll tell him it tore on the way here. We'll tell him I burnt it while ironing it.'

'This is my mistake. Remember he made us sign a contract? There was a line about wearing what they asked you to wear. I'd thought *how bad could it be*, and signed it off. Sorry, but you'll have to wear this,' said Moin's mother.

'Maybe it really won't fit,' said Moin hopefully.

'You have to go for a dress rehearsal tomorrow morning,' Moin's father reminded him. 'Are Tony and Parvati coming?'

'No, they have better things to do,' said Moin bitterly.

This was all the monster's fault. If it had not refused to sing Loopy's song, Moin would not have had to sing instead and Loopy would not have sent the potion and the monster would not have disappeared. Now that the monster was gone, not only did Moin have to deal with all the bananas, he also had no choice but to wear a terrible costume and sing at the concert himself.

The monster was a menace when it was around and a menace when it was not.

THE BIG CONCERT

In school, everyone was talking about the concert. Surprisingly, many people actually liked Loopy Bagiri's songs. Older kids kept coming to Moin and asking him to sing this or that song of Loopy's. But Moin did not know any of the songs. The only song of Loopy's he knew was the one he was going to sing at the concert. He hated it.

Moin's music teacher Tothogotho Choudhury hated Loopy's music too. If he had a choice, he would have told Moin not to sing at the concert. Moin was his favourite student, and it pained him to have him sing Loopy's horrible songs. But he could not say this to anyone, because his wife, who was Loopy's sister, would be very upset if he did.

Tothogotho came personally to apologize to Mr and Mrs Kaif for putting Moin in this position.

'If Moin had not had that throat problem at my concert, none of this would have happened,' he said sadly.

He was being kind, felt Mr and Mrs Kaif. Moin's horrible singing at the concert could hardly be dismissed as a throat problem. What about the terrible tune? And the awful lyrics?

But they nodded and smiled and assured Mr Choudhury that they did not hold him responsible.

The day of the concert came. To Moin's deep disappointment, there was no cyclone or earthquake or any other natural disaster. Mr and Mrs Kaif sighed sadly when Moin was not around.

It was a particularly pleasant day, so there was quite a crowd at the venue. The advantage of this was that Mr and Mrs Kaif could blend into the crowd and no one would know that Moin was their son.

The disadvantage was that thousands of people would hear Moin sing. Since they loved their son despite his terrible singing, they were upset that people with good taste would laugh at him. Eatables were not allowed in the auditorium, so at least he'd be spared rotten tomatoes. But everyone was wearing shoes, Mr Kaif noticed in alarm.

Moin was itchy in his new costume. All kinds of shiny things stitched on to it made the insides really scratchy. And all the chains he had to wear made him jangle every time he moved. He tried telling his dresser that he would get confused between the jangling of the chains and the jingling of the music, but the dresser acted like he couldn't hear a word Moin said.

Or maybe the chains are jangling so loudly that no one can hear anything over it, thought Moin.

Moin was really worried about the concert. When he went on stage to sing in Tothogotho

Choudhury's concert, he hadn't been worried at all. He knew the songs, he enjoyed singing them. But Loopy's song was very hard to sing, and so many things could go wrong.

He hoped he would remember the ridiculous words.

He hoped he wouldn't mess up the ridiculous tune.

Worst of all, he had to sing in that false screechy voice that Loopy had made him practise. It made his throat feel like someone had pushed sandpaper down it.

As he sat alone in the dressing room, waiting for his cue to go on stage, for the first time, Moin really wished the monster was back. Then it could do the singing, and he could just mime the words. He hated Loopy's songs and he hated his costume and he hated singing in a monster-like voice. And his friends hadn't even come to see him.

As if thinking about them had conjured them up, Tony and Parvati poked their heads round the door.

'Hey, Monster Songster, why are you looking like you swallowed a lemon and it turned out to be a tennis ball?' asked Parvati.

'It's very odd,' said Moin. 'I suddenly miss the monster.'

'I miss it all the time!' declared Tony.

'That's only because you want to complete the book and the list of rules,' retorted Moin. 'It used to drive me nuts with its singing and the bananas and the nonsense it kept talking. You guys could go home, but I had to live with it. And yet, suddenly I wish—'

'MOIN!' shouted someone outside his room. 'YOU'RE UP NEXT!'

Moin nearly tripped on his ridiculous costume as he rushed out. Parvati and Tony went with him up to the edge of the stage.

As they waited for Moin to be called on to the stage, Parvati asked him in a whisper, 'What do you wish? You didn't finish!'

'I wish—'

'And let's welcome the new sensation, the Monster Songster—'

'—the monster—'

'MO-IIII-N KAIF!'

'—would come back!' said Moin as he stepped on to the stage.

'Took you long enough,' said a voice in Moin's pocket.

MONSTER RULE 411

If a monster disappears, the only thing that can make it appear is a wish made by the child who drew it into the world.

A New Song

Moin the Monster Songster was an instant sensation.

But no one was pleased.

Mr and Mrs Kaif were unhappy because they had been hoping that this concert would be a flop. That way, they would have stuck to the agreement they had signed with Loopy, and yet they'd have been free of Loopy for good. Now Loopy might want to do more of these concerts with Moin. Mrs Kaif shuddered at the thought. Mr Kaif chewed the brim of his hat in distress.

Loopy was unhappy because Moin had not sung the song he was supposed to. The monster, of course, had sung its own song. People were raving about this new song. Only Loopy and Moin knew that it was not Loopy's song.

This was the song Moin was supposed to sing:

Yellow man!
Yellow man!
What a super fellow, man!

He's a first-class singer
He is awesome when he sings
How handsome yellow fellow looks
With all his chains and rings!
He's good as gold and that is why
He wears those golden things!

Yeah!

Yellow man!
Yellow man!
What a splendid fellow
Man!

Yellow man!
Yellow man!
Awesome, super, splendid, first-class
Yellow fellow man!

And this is what the monster sang:

Where did I go,
I don't know

*Nor does anyone else.
All I know is a
Rum-pum-po
And a rum-pum never tells.*

*A rum-rum-po!
A rum-rum-po!
A rum-pum never tells!
It will not if you ask it soft,
And never if you yell.*

*Where did I go,
I don't know
And I don't really care.
All I know is
A bum-bum-bear
And a bum-bum is nowhere.*

*A bum-bum-bear!
A bum-bum-bear!
A bum-bum is nowhere!
It does not live upon the land
And is not in the air.*

*Where did I go,
I don't know
But now I sing a song.
All I know is
A ding-ding-doo
And a ding-ding cannot dong.*

A ding-ding-doo!
A ding-ding-doo!
A ding-ding cannot dong!
But if you want a ding to dong
Then you must play ping-pong.

Hey!
A ding-ding-dong!
A ding-ding-dong!
A ding-ding-ding-ding-dong!
A ding-ding-dong!
A ding-ding-dong!
A ding-ding-ping-ping-pong!

As always, the audience erupted when the monster sang, singing and dancing along, so no one noticed that Moin was struggling to lip-sync with the monster's silly song.

Mr and Mrs Kaif were trying to hide under their chairs, so they didn't notice either.

Parvati and Tony were looking at each other in horror, so they didn't notice either. All they knew was that Moin seemed to have pretty much become the monster, musically speaking. He sounded *exactly* like the monster. Since Loopy loved the monster's voice, it meant that Loopy would ask Moin to sing more songs for him. Which meant that they would have to—as loyal friends—go to more of these ear-shattering events.

So they were unhappy too.

Sitting in the car on his way home, Moin didn't know whether to be happy or miserable. On the happy side, he hadn't had to sing that terrible song Loopy had written for him. But on the unhappy side, he'd had to endure the monster shrieking close to his ear. And now it looked like he might have to keep singing for Loopy. He only hoped Loopy would be so ticked off that he hadn't sung what he was supposed to sing that he would not ask him to sing again.

The monster's return was the thing that he was not sure about. Was he happy or unhappy?

The monster, after the concert, was strangely quiet. It did look a little pale, Moin felt. Almost transparent. As if it hadn't fully appeared yet. And he couldn't talk to it because his parents were with him.

He wished he could just tell them about the monster. But he couldn't. They would definitely freak out.

Moin, Tony and Parvati had talked about telling them once, before the monster's disappearance.

'No! They'll take it away and give it off to the police or the zoo or to scientists who study aliens!' Tony had exclaimed, when Parvati suggested it.

'There's a rule about that,' had said the monster.

MONSTER RULE 59

If the monster is taken away from its child, terrible things might happen to the child.

'That doesn't sound like a rule at all,' said Moin suspiciously.

'I might have got the words wrong. Maybe it's "horrible" and not "terrible".'

And now, in the silence of the car, Moin began to wonder if he'd made a big mistake when he'd wished the monster would come back.

But then a happy thought struck him: his banana problem was now solved!

IT'S BAAACK!

The monster ate eight bananas the next day.

Moin's mother was a bit alarmed. 'Maybe we should check Moin for worms,' she told Mr Kaif. 'How is he eating so many bananas?'

But Mr Kaif, who was getting a bit tired of looking for new banana recipes on the net, was very happy at this turn of events.

'No, no,' he said quickly. 'Bananas are good for him. All that, erm, magnesium, you know. Or maybe it's potassium? Anyway, they're very good.'

Mrs Kaif was not fully convinced. She decided to keep a close watch on Moin. But Moin seemed okay, even though he'd taken to singing in that horrible voice again. She blamed that on Loopy and on the sudden fame that Loopy's concert had brought Moin.

The day after the concert was a Sunday, and the Kaifs' doorbell and mobile phones would not stop ringing. People they barely knew were calling to congratulate Moin on his grand success. Forgotten relatives came bearing flowers and fruit and chocolates for Moin. Mr and Mrs Kaif were stunned. They had no idea that there were so many people with such bad taste in music.

Their neighbours, Mr and Mrs Sharma, who used to turn up their noses at the Kaifs, came with laddoos and insisted on giving them to Moin themselves. Moin had to eat three laddoos in quick succession. They were not

even very good. After they left, he burped in cardamom flavour continuously for fifteen minutes.

Mr Screwwala, who had once complained to the residents' association about the noise that came from Moin's bedroom, showed up with a packet of frozen peas.

'I come in peace!' he declared, as he handed the packet to Moin. 'Peas, peace, get it?' he asked with a cackle. 'How was I to know that the cacophony that emerged from the young lad's room was a precursor to such fame? Huh? It sounded to me like the caterwauling of cats, but what do I know? Now every time I open YouTube, all I can hear is "Ding-Ding-Dong" by Moin, our very own Monster Songster! Well done, well done, well done!'

He looked so pleased that Moin didn't have the heart to tell him that the frozen packet was giving him frostbite. And after he left, Moin found that the peas were past their expiry date. He threw them into the waste bin.

Where the monster found them a little later, when it managed to escape from Moin's room and sneak into the kitchen to look for bananas.

Moin was in his room, searching in a panic for the missing monster, when it came back dragging the packet of peas, open now, and

half empty. The monster's hair was covered in chewed bits of peas, so it was not hard to figure out what had happened to half the peas.

'Why did you eat those!' Moin exclaimed. 'They're past the use-by date! Something could happen to you!'

'Nothing will happen because dates mean nothing to me. Not the kind of dates you eat, of course. Those mean a lot. In fact, I made up a song about them:

Dates are delicious,
Dates are fine,

Dates are the best things
To ea-ea-eat!

Dates are squishious,
Dates are prime,
But the best thing is
Dates are swee-ee-eet!

Dates are—

'Gah! Stop!' cried Moin.
　'Why? It's not even over yet. Listen. The third stanza goes like this:

Dates are—

'STOP!' Moin yelled. 'You want to know why? Okay, I'll tell you why. In fact, I'll tell you many whys: why one, because it's a stupid, idiotic, horrible song; why two, because my parents will come to see what's going on if you keep on with that racket; why three—and that's the most important why—because you haven't finished what you were saying. What do you mean dates mean nothing to you?'
　'Uff. What a stupid boy. It's simple enough. Monsters don't believe in time. So we have no dates. There's even a rule about that.'

Moin was so stunned that he could not speak for five whole minutes. The monster took the chance to finish off the aged frozen peas.

'Can I have some more?' it asked.

Luckily, the bell rang again. This time, it was Tony. He had come to spend the afternoon, while his parents took his grandfather to see an old friend at the other end of town.

As soon as Tony came into the room, Moin burst out, 'It says there is no such thing as time!'

Tony looked at Moin, aghast. He had been a bit worried about Moin ever since the concert the previous night. Something had clearly gone wrong with his friend. Otherwise, why would he sing that stupid song in that horrible voice? And now, here he was, talking utter gibberish. Moin seemed to think that someone had said that *time* did not exist!

MONSTER RULE 579

There is no such thing as time.

If Moin had been a deep, thoughtful kind of kid who pondered over questions of time and space and existence, Tony might not have been so concerned. But this was Moin, who was the kind of kid who, if asked, 'What is time?', was most likely to say 'Four o'clock.' Something was definitely amiss.

He decided to break up Moin's unexpected statement into small bits to make it easier.

'Who says?' asked Tony, for starters.

'I say,' said the monster from under the bed.

The monster was chewing at its hair to get at the bits of peas stuck in it, so its voice sounded muffled and stranger than usual.

Tony jumped.

'What was that?' he tried to say, but all that came out of his throat was a croak.

'Have you turned into a frog?' asked the monster, sticking its grinning head out from under the bed.

Tony was so happy to see the monster that he started babbling. 'When? How? What? Where were you? We got so worried when you disappeared! And now? How? How did you come back? Say something!'

'I didn't get a chance to tell you,' began Moin. But the monster cut him off with a song, which it sang standing on top of a pile of books on Moin's table:

I'm back, I'm back
I'm baaaack!
I was there but now I am here!

I'm back, I'm back
I'm baaaack!
I was far but now I am near!

I'm back, I'm back
I'm baaaack!
I sang a song on the stage!

I'm back, I'm back
I'm baaaack!
And now I am all the rage!

I'm back, I'm back
I'm baaaack!
With a swagger, a swash and a swish!

I'm back, I'm back
I'm baaaack!
Because that was Moin's wiiiiishhh!!

'Yup!' said Moin, nodding gloomily. 'That's pretty much what happened.'

Papaya Cake

'That's not even possible,' said Parvati.

Tony and Moin had felt that they needed to have a serious meeting to talk about this new monster rule, so they had made a phone call to Parvati's house. Parvati was not happy to have been pulled out of her violin class for this.

But when her teacher heard that it was Moin who was calling her, he insisted on letting her go.

'Ayyo, that boy! He will be very famous. Bad voice and all, but what that matters? He is singing for Loopy sir! Please, when you see Moin, ask if I can play violin for Loopy sir, please, uh?'

By the time Parvati got to Moin's house, she was upset with Moin, Tony, her parents and her violin teacher. So when she saw the monster, she scowled at it and said, 'Ha! I should have known.'

Since no one knew what she should have known, they ignored her remark and told her about the new monster rule.

'That's not possible,' said Parvati, with the confidence of someone whose uncle was a scientist. 'Whether you believe it or not, time exists. And I can prove it.'

The monster smirked. 'It doesn't matter if you can prove it or not. A rule is a rule. There might even be a rule about proving things. Let me try and remember it.'

Even Tony, who wrote down all the monster rules diligently, could see that the monster was making that one up.

'But don't you see?' he said to Parvati, who was scowling so hard that her eyebrows had scrunched up into a small hill over her nose. 'If there is no time in monsterland, then maybe it can go back and forth in human time! So maybe my theory is right, after all. Maybe it's a time traveller!'

'What's a monsterland?' asked the monster.

'Where you come from,' explained Tony. 'It's another word for monster world.'

'I don't come from a place.'

'Now it'll say space does not exist,' said Parvati snarkily.

'Exactly!' said the monster happily. 'No such thing as space. I think there's a rule.'

'But . . . But . . . But . . .' Tony floundered.

'I told you,' Moin said morosely. 'All those rules are just made up. None of them are true.'

'But what about rule number 83?' reminded Tony.

MONSTER RULE 83

Monsters cannot lie.

'Actually, that space thing might not be a rule, I just felt that it should be,' the monster said. 'But the time one absolutely is. I might have got it wrong though. Maybe it says: There is no such thing as a timetable. Or timepiece. Or time bomb. Or time out. Or—'

There was a knock at the door. Mr Kaif came in with a plate full of some gooey lumps. 'Papaya cake!' he declared proudly.

Moin remembered seeing a squishy-looking papaya that one of his aunts had brought as a gift. Why anyone would think that he would want a papaya, he didn't know. And why his father would think of making a cake with it, he had no idea.

Parvati and Tony tried to look pleased about the lumps of papaya cake. But Moin could see that they were having trouble keeping the smiles on their faces, so he quickly took the plate and thanked his father.

As Mr Kaif turned to go, he caught a glimpse of pink. But when he turned around, he saw it was nothing but a drawing on Moin's desk. 'Er, nice drawing, Moin,' he said, sounding slightly sad.

As he later told Mrs Kaif with a sigh, 'Moin can't draw. Or sing. Never mind. There are other things he can do. Maybe he'll become a chef. He might get my talent for cooking.'

Mrs Kaif really hoped not. The pot of periwinkle in the balcony had been fed a lump of papaya cake. She would have to dig it out later, because she was not sure the periwinkles would survive it. If Moin started cooking like his father, she might have to eat raw vegetables for the rest of her life.

But Mr Kaif was so proud of his papaya cake, she didn't have the heart to say anything. So she nodded and smiled, and drank another glass of water to get the horrible taste out of her mouth. She decided never to let another papaya inside the house.

Back in Moin's room, the three of them were looking in horror at the lumps on the plate.

'Do we *have* to eat it?' asked Tony anxiously.

'I have an idea!' said Parvati. She turned to the monster. It was trying to stand on top of a table lamp. 'Hey, you want some cake?'

Moin was not sure this was a good idea. 'There's that rule about human food,' he reminded Parvati.

'Rule number 112,' said Tony, who had written them all down and knew them like the back of his hand.

MONSTER RULE 112

Food fit for humans is not always fit for monsters.

But the monster had hopped off the lamp and was staring at the plate greedily.

'Hang on!' said Parvati, holding the plate out of the monster's reach. 'We'll play a game. We'll ask you a question, and if you answer it, you get a lump . . . er . . . a piece of cake. Agreed?'

Moin and Tony gasped in admiration. This was a brilliant plan. Now maybe they would be able to figure out where the monster had gone when it disappeared.

But getting the monster to answer questions was easier said than done. It would not sit quiet long enough to be asked a question. It was so excited at the thought of eating gooey cake that it began to sing and dance.

Ask a silly question,
Get a silly answer,
Coz I am a singer
And a dilly dancer.

Dilly-dilly-dilly,
I'm a dilly dancer,
Silly-silly question
And a silly answer.

'Stop!' yelled Parvati. 'Do you want the cake or not? If you do, you have to sit down! Stop dancing!'

'I can't stop. I'm an artist, and I have to express myself through my art. You can ask questions while I dance.'

So while they asked questions, the monster danced and whirled and swung and be-bopped. At least it had stopped singing. Moin had been worried that his parents would come to see what was going on if the monster had gone on screeching.

'Where were you when you disappeared?' asked Tony.

'Dunno,' said the monster, as it did a cartwheel.

'Why did you take so long to come back?' asked Moin.

'Because you didn't wish me back,' it said, shimmying past Moin.

'But you must have been nearby if you heard me wish for you. You could have told me you were around.'

'But I wasn't.' It was rotating really fast on its head now. Tony was taking notes. It would all go into his book on the strange behaviour of monsters.

'Don't be silly. How could you have heard him if you were not nearby?' asked Parvati.

'What do you mean by nearby? What is nearby to you might be far out to me. And I might be near enough to hear but too far to see,' the monster said, doing a ballet stretch.

'Uff,' huffed Parvati. 'Such nonsense.'

But Tony was interested. 'That sounds like a conundrum!' he said.

'No, it does not,' said Moin. 'It sounds like a riddle, not like a drum. A drum is much louder and goes dum-dum-dum. Unless it goes tok-tok-tok. What kind of drum is a conun? I've never heard of it.'

'Conundrum means riddle,' Tony explained. 'Maybe it's giving us a clue. Near enough to hear but too far to see.'

'Thunder!' said Moin excitedly.

'Thunder is not a place. You can't be in or at thunder,' Parvati pointed out.

'Oh. Then I have no idea. Maybe it meant too far to sea? Like s-e-a, not s-e-e?'

'And how does that help?' asked Parvati. 'The sea is so far away that it's definitely not near enough to hear.'

'Okay, we give up,' said Tony, turning to the monster. 'Where's near enough to hear but too far to see?'

But while they were talking, the monster had managed to get to the plate of sticky papaya cake lumps and had stuffed them all in its mouth, so it could not say a word until it was time for Parvati and Tony to go home.

Bus Ride

'Two days?' Mrs Kaif was not at all happy.

Moin's school often took the children on field trips. It was usually just a day trip to some nearby park, but this time they were going to a hill station and would stay overnight.

'What about your worms? Where will you get bananas? What if you fall off the mountain?' She was so worried that she was hopping from one unlikely problem to the other, as she walked round and round the room agitatedly.

'Worms? What worms?' asked Moin. He had not heard about his mother's worm theory based on his excessive banana eating.

'Did I say worms? I meant germs,' Mrs Kaif said quickly. 'These hill stations are full of germs.' As soon as she said it, she realized how

little sense it made, so she collapsed into an armchair. 'It's too dangerous,' she whispered to herself.

But she also knew she was being unreasonable. And so, two days later, Moin was all packed and waiting at school for the bus that would take them on their trip.

'What did you do with it?' hissed Tony, in such a loud whisper that Mrs Kaif heard him.

'With what?' she asked suspiciously.

'Er, um, there was a drawing that Moin did that I wanted to see,' Tony stuttered.

Mrs Kaif smiled lovingly at Tony. Moin was so lucky to have such loyal friends, she felt. Anyone who actually wanted to see a drawing done by Moin must really love him. There could be no other explanation. She loved her son, but even she could see how horrible Moin's drawings were.

There was particularly one that he seemed to really like. Maybe he was trying to draw someone or the other, but it looked like no creature Mrs Kaif had ever seen. And it was pink! But Moin seemed oddly attached to it. He was forever looking at it, and once or twice she suspected that he was even talking to it. Like an imaginary friend. She had read that only children often made up imaginary friends.

So when she had been about to zip up his suitcase, she put the drawing of the pink creature right under all his clothes, as a happy surprise for him. *He won't want to go away for three days without his special friend*, she'd thought, patting Moin on the head fondly in her mind.

Waiting for a trip to start always made Moin strangely anxious. So it took him a second, but he finally understood what Tony was trying to ask.

'I left it in the room, inside the cupboard, with lots of bananas,' Moin said out of the corner of his mouth.

'Thank goodness,' whispered Parvati. 'Otherwise we'd have to hear it singing all through the trip.'

The bus finally arrived, and all the children got on. Once they had settled and the bus got going, Mrs Kapur (with one U) clapped her hands and said, 'Let's sing some songs!'

'Ding-ding-dong!!' everyone shouted.

Moin's heart sank. He'd have to do a monster imitation again.

'Let's sing something else,' said Parvati, correctly guessing Moin's thoughts. Also, she had no desire to hear that horrible song.

So they sang some other songs, but after a while, Mrs Kapuur (with two Us), who was a big Loopy fan, said, 'Moin, beta, sing it once, for us. When we have such a star with us, how can he not sing, right, Mrs K?'

Mrs Kapur, who was quite in awe of Mrs Kapuur, said, 'Of course, Mrs Kapuur! Moin, when miss is asking you to sing, you cannot say no!'

Looking as miserable as he felt, Moin began to sing the song. But he need not have worried. As soon as he started singing, everyone joined in so loudly that he did not even need to sing.

He just had to lip-sync, and he had got very good at that. He noticed, to his amazement, that someone in the bus sang just like the monster.

He got up from his seat and craned his neck as he looked around, trying to figure out who it was who had exactly the same voice as the monster. That's when he noticed that Tony and Parvati were looking up with expressions of deep alarm. What were they looking at, though? What was on the ceiling of the bus?

He nudged Parvati with his elbow.

'Ow!' she shouted. Then, 'It's here!' she whisper-shrieked, pointing up at Moin's suitcase on the luggage rack above her head, which was doing a sort of dance. Moin's stomach did a double somersault.

He could not stop lip-syncing now, so until the song got over, Tony, Parvati and Moin sat with their eyes fixed on the dancing suitcase.

Finally, the song got over and everyone applauded loudly. But Moin continued to look upwards in shock.

'Such concentration! Such dedication,' said Mrs Kapuur, giving Moin a hug and wiping the tears of appreciation that had come to her eyes. 'It's the sign of a true artist.'

Everyone then settled down for a nap. But Moin was gasping.

'Are you having a panic attack?' Tony asked in concern.

Moin shook his head.

'Then why are you breathing like that?' asked Parvati.

'I'b tryig dot to breathe!' Moin said. He was now holding his nose with one hand and waving his other hand in front of his face.

When he had calmed down, he whispered, 'Lavender perfume!'

'Ah!' Tony and Parvati got it at once.

When they were little and had just become friends, they had once got stuck in a cupboard at Parvati's house. In the scuffle and panic, they had managed to break a bottle of lavender perfume. Ever since then, the three of them hated the smell, but Moin most of all.

Lavender was Mrs Kapuur's favourite perfume.

The three had a quick conference: should they get the monster out of the suitcase while everyone was asleep? Or was it better to let it stay there till they reached?

'I thought you left it in the cupboard at home?' asked Parvati.

'Yes, with bananas! I don't know how it got out. Sometimes I think it knows magic.'

'Maybe it does!' said Tony, his eyes shining at the thought.

'If it did,' said the practical Parvati, 'it would have got out of the suitcase magically. Must have slipped out through a crack using the flattening trick.'

That did seem the most likely answer to Moin. They had more or less decided to let the monster stay in the suitcase, when it let out a loud shriek—

'LET ME OUT!'

Luckily, at that very moment, the driver braked suddenly, and half the children fell off their seats. In the general screaming and howling, no one noticed the monster's shriek.

The helper in the bus announced, 'Ten minutes toilet stop!'

Everyone got out of the bus, but Moin, Tony and Parvati stayed inside. They quickly took down the suitcase and opened it. Out popped the monster.

'How did you get in there?' asked Moin.

'Magic!' said the monster.

THE CALL 1

Principal K.K. Kuttykrishnan (popularly known as Kooki) had been feeling much better of late. But that day, for some reason, he had been thinking of Boeing and of Dr Reddy.

He had not gone back to Dr Reddy in a long time; though his last visit to the man had been quite fruitful.

'I am very proud of you for trying to save this boy, despite your hostility towards him,' Dr Reddy had told him.

'But I don't have any hosti—' Kooki had begun, but then he remembered that saying that would mean he was in denial. He didn't know what else to say.

He was rather confused. Every time he encountered the boy Boeing (for some reason he could never remember his real name), something strange happened. Either he heard weird songs, or he saw pink things. The last time, admittedly, there was nothing pink in sight, but there was that buzzing fuzzy thing that the boy and his friend Tony (for some reason he always remembered *his* name) were running after on the street.

'Did you consider the possibility that this buzzing "thing" was just a toy aeroplane?'

'Boeing!' cackled Kooki, struck by the idea of Boeing the boy running after Boeing the aeroplane. He found it so funny that he cackled for two minutes without pause. Kooki had an active, if slightly strange, sense of humour.

Dr Reddy looked at him in fascination and excitedly took notes. He thanked his luck for having got such an interesting case study. He had already written a paper about Kooki (name changed, of course) which had been published in the journal *Mind Matters* to great acclaim. But there was enough material here to write a book! He would call it *Master Mind: Inside the Head of a Stressed Educator.* Dr Reddy congratulated himself on a really catchy title. He was sure it was going to be a bestseller.

Kooki sobered down suddenly. 'Yes, yes, quite possible. Maybe it was just a toy aeroplane. So Teacher and I managed to disperse the crowds,' he told Dr Reddy,

a little untruthfully, because it was Mrs Kooki's umbrella that had done the job.

Dr Reddy was looking a little more baffled than usual at the sudden introduction of this new character. 'Teacher?' he asked faintly, his pen poised over his notebook.

'Haha! Anh, my wife, you know, Doctor. I call her Teacher only. And she calls me Sir. Very romantic, no?' Kooki asked coyly.

The word that came to Dr Reddy's mind was not 'romantic' but 'demented'.

But he was a very good psychiatrist, so he smiled and nodded and said, 'Yes, indeed! So you and . . . er . . . Teacher managed to get rid of the people who were bothering the children?'

Kooki had an attack of conscience. 'Actually, it was all Teacher's doing,' he admitted. 'She used her umbrella. That umbrella is too good!' He shook his head admiringly. 'The crowd just disappeared, like that!' he said, clicking his fingers. 'I tried talking to them, but what was the use. Enh? It was like that saying in Hindi, something about kicking a ghost, anh?'

'A . . . a ghost?' gasped Dr Reddy. His notebook was filling up really fast. He had no idea how ghosts and phantoms had come into the conversation, but it was rich material for his book.

'Ayyo, that saying, no, in Hindi, about ghosts and kicking and talking. You know the one, doctor. Tch. I can't remember exactly. Teacher will know. Her Hindi is very good.'

Dr Reddy's Hindi was limited to a few phrases he'd picked up from Hindi films.

One was '*Main kahan hoon?*' which is what the hero or heroine said whenever they lost their memory, which happened more frequently than was possible.

The other was '*Koi mujhe bachao!*' because every heroine in every Hindi movie he'd seen needed to be rescued at some point.

Right then, Dr Reddy was vacillating between the two options. He would have liked very much to be rescued from this patient, but that was unworthy of a psychiatrist. So he said instead, '*Main kahan hoon?*'

Kooki had stared at Dr Reddy. 'I think I should go now!' he said in alarm.

Dr Reddy had not disagreed. His hand was cramping from the rapid writing, and his head was spinning. He really had a moment of not knowing where he was.

So Kooki had rushed out. He popped his head back in a moment later: 'The ghost of kicks won't submit to talks,' he had said with a huge smile on his face. 'Suddenly remembered!' Then he left with a jaunty wave.

Dr Reddy had immediately cancelled all his remaining appointments for the day to try and decipher that riddle.

Though slightly strange, the session had done Kooki a lot of good. He'd come home feeling cheerful and happy. The buzzing creature was a toy aeroplane, and there had been no pink-creature sightings after that visit to Moin's house. So maybe what he had seen hanging on the clothesline there was, as Teacher said, a piece of paper with the drawing of a pink creature on it.

'It was a very bad drawing, Teacher,' he now told his wife with a shudder, as they sat sipping filter coffee and talking about this and that. 'Very bad. That boy cannot draw. He should not be allowed to draw!'

'Come, come, Sir,' said his wife gently. 'As teachers, we should not judge our students' work like that. Who knows, when he grows up,

he might become a great artist. I'm sure Picasso was also told he was very bad at drawing when he was a child. Look at those faces he draws. They don't look like human beings. Yet, he became so famous.'

'Anh, you're right, Teacher. Becoming famous nowadays has nothing to do with being talented, enh? You heard that Boeing boy's new song, no? So famous it has become. Good only we didn't go.' He shuddered again, remembering that voice. It was the same voice that he thought he had heard in his office one day. It had given him many nightmares.

Kooki's wife sighed. She had really wanted to go to Loopy Bagiri's concert to hear Moin sing. But she felt Kooki might get traumatized again. At the last concert, he had become very agitated. He kept talking about something pink. That boy Moin was a sweet boy, but, for some reason, he had a very bad effect on Sir. So she had agreed that they would not go.

The song was everywhere now. It was a terrible song, yes, but it would have been nice to sit in the front row at the concert and tell everyone proudly that the singer was a student in her husband's school.

Both Kooki and his wife were thinking of Moin, therefore, when the call came.

THE CALL 2

Mrs Kaif was trying to do a particularly hard t'ai chi pose.

Whenever she got anxious, she did t'ai chi. It made her muscles groan and ache, so it took her mind off all her other anxieties.

She had had a really bad night. Someone at the office strongly recommended a film. Usually, she did not have the time for movies, but with Moin away in the mountains, she needed a distraction. It was clear pretty early on that it was the wrong movie to watch when she was already worried about her son falling off a mountain.

The movie was about a young man falling into a gorge.

But once she started watching it, she could not stop because it was such an exciting, nail-biting film. Every bit as good as her colleague had said it would be. She sat with a cushion on her face and peered over it every few seconds to see if it had got a little less scary.

Mr Kaif could not understand it. 'Why don't you just switch it off?' he asked. 'You'll only make yourself more nervous.'

'No!' yelled Mrs Kaif. 'I need to know how it ends!'

Fortunately for her peace of mind, it ended well. The young man was rescued and they all lived happily ever after.

But after that, she could not sleep.

'What if he decides to go exploring with his two friends?' she said, sitting up in bed suddenly. 'And falls into a chasm?'

'The teachers won't let them go anywhere,' Mr Kaif said drowsily.

'That's true,' Mrs Kaif assured herself and tried to sleep again. But just as she dozed off, she dreamt of Moin falling into a crevice. For some reason, he had the drawing of that strange pink creature in his hand and was singing Loopy's horrible song as he fell.

She woke up screaming. And she wasn't sure if it was the drawing, the song or the fall that made her scream the most.

Mr Kaif got her a glass of Horlicks. He was a great believer in Horlicks. It was his go-to solution for constipation, loose motion, gas, hunger and insomnia.

Mrs Kaif hated Horlicks. But she was so shaken by her nightmare that she drank it up without a murmur. Then she burped all night and couldn't sleep.

So in the morning, tired and groggy, she decided to do some t'ai chi.

Mrs Kaif loved t'ai chi. The movements were so graceful and slow and majestic.

She first finished Waving Hands Like Clouds. Then she decided to Wave Hands Like Clouds to Repulse Monkey.

She considered White Goose Spreads Wings but decided she would Grasp Sparrow's Tail first, because that kind of followed from Waving Hands Like Clouds and Repulsing Monkey.

Then she did White Goose (she preferred it to White Crane, somehow, though it was the same thing) and then Carried Tiger to Mountain. This always intrigued her. *Why couldn't Tiger climb Mountain by itself*, she wondered, as she pivoted slowly and gracefully on her left foot.

She had tried to understand how these movements had been named. Maybe some t'ai chi master had to Carry Tiger to Mountain once. It could have happened. Then they must have recreated the movements and

taught them to generations of t'ai chi students. Otherwise, why Tiger? Why not Carry Cheetah to Mountain? Or Lion? Or Panther?

She moved on to the Golden Rooster Standing on Left Leg and felt a moment of great peace. Then she changed fluidly to Fair Lady Works Shuttles.

It was while she was Creeping Low Like a Snake that she got the call.

MISSING!

Mrs Kapuur and Mrs Kapur herded all the children into the bus with the help of Albert Bhaiyya, the staffroom assistant from school who had come with them.

They were screeching with excitement after their morning out. They had left early, had breakfast in a restaurant on the main mall road and then wandered through the market, buying things and making faces at the monkeys on the parapets and roofs. They were now headed to a botanical garden for a nature walk.

The bus started moving while Mrs Kapur called out the children's names. But they were so loud that she couldn't hear their responses.

'Just do a headcount, Mrs Kapur,' said Mrs Kapuur.

'What a good idea, Mrs Kapuur!' said Mrs Kapur.

She started counting the heads she could see. They were five short. Then she looked under the seats and counted some more heads. They were still three short.

Panicking slightly, she went through the list and started ticking off names, starting from the first seat and going right up to the back of the bus.

Still three missing! And when she looked at the list again, she froze.

'Mrs Kapuuuuuur,' she called in a squeaky whisper.

'What is it? What?' asked Mrs Kapuur sharply.

'M-missing children,' gasped Mrs Kapur, feeling quite faint.

'Children? Plural? Come on, Mrs K, don't faint now. Tell me, how many missing?'

Mrs Kapur held up the sheets and pointed out the three unticked names.

'Oh my goodness! STOOOOOOPPP!' shouted Mrs Kapuur to the driver.

When Mrs Kapuur was a little girl, her twin brothers called her gunthroat because she had such a loud voice. She had tried to tone down her voice, but then she realized that they were just jealous, because they both had thin, reedy

voices. So she'd stopped trying to make her voice smaller and, instead, exercised her voice to make it stronger and louder. She was always picked for debates because she could outvoice her opponents, and she was always the drillmaster for the Republic Day parade in her college.

So, when Mrs Kapuur shouted 'STOP!', not only their bus, but all the vehicles on the road screeched to a halt.

This was not the best thing to happen on a mountain road. Everyone started honking and shouting. The vehicles going up started rolling backwards; the vehicles going down started rolling forwards. Some ambitious drivers tried to overtake others. There was complete and total chaos for many minutes. Then a policeman came with a loud whistle and created some more confusion.

Meanwhile, Mrs Kapuur was yelling at the hapless driver of their bus. 'TURN AROUUUND AT ONCE!'

The driver was called Chhotu, because he must have, long long ago, been small. People forget that all small children grow up and stop being small, and this was particularly true in Chhotu's case, because Chhotu was rather big. But years of being called small had made Chhotu timid.

His eyes filled with tears. He was reminded of his old gran who used to shout at him like that when he was a little toddler left in her care, while his mother took the goats to graze.

'But I can't turn, modom,' he said mournfully. 'Narrow roads, modom, no place. And traffic jam, modom.'

'OUR CHILDREN ARE MISSING! WE HAVE TO GO BACK NOW!' shouted Mrs Kapuur.

A few more people on the road went deaf.

Mrs Kapur tapped Mrs Kapuur lightly on the shoulder. 'Mrs Kapuur, can I suggest something? One of us should get down and go back to the mall, and one of us, along with Albert, can take these children to the garden.'

Mrs Kapuur panted as she thought about this and caught her breath. 'Good idea,' she said finally. 'But please be careful, okay? Keep on counting heads!'

She hopped out of the bus, crossed the road and got into a random vehicle going in the opposite direction. 'MARKET ROAD!' she shouted, and the driver meekly took her there as soon as the traffic started moving. Anything to stop the scary woman from shouting in his ear.

Mrs Kapuur got off, fully expecting to see the three missing children sitting by the road, looking frightened and sorry.

But though the road was milling with all kinds of people, Moin, Tony and Parvati were nowhere around.

The road was strangely quiet, too. There were people talking, vehicles honking and hawkers calling out their wares loudly, so at first Mrs Kapuur didn't know why she got the feeling that it was quiet.

Then she noticed that there were no monkeys.

When they were here earlier, there had been monkeys everywhere! One of them had even grabbed her goggles. But Mrs Bulbul

Kapuur was not afraid of a mere monkey. She had thought for a moment, then had taken out a little shiny keychain from her bag.

'Here, monkey!' she had said. 'Take this and give me my glasses.'

The monkey had been so excited to see the shiny thing that he had thrown Mrs Kapuur's glasses to the ground in contempt. It seemed a measly thing in comparison to the shiny object dangling in front of his eyes.

Mrs Kapuur had totally focused on the monkey. Just when it seemed like he was about to leap at her, she had thrown the keychain in the opposite direction, and dived to the ground to pick up her glasses.

One of the lenses was missing, but, luckily, Mrs Kapur had spotted it earlier and had quickly picked it up. The frame was still intact, so Mrs Kapuur had popped the lens back into the frame, popped the goggles back on her face and sailed away, while all her students had clapped. It had been quite a triumphant moment.

She had had a large audience of monkeys and humans then. But now, the only monkey she could see was a particularly old fellow with a cunning look. He seemed to know something, but since she didn't speak monkey-tongue, she couldn't ask him what.

Instead, she went from shop to shop, asking if anyone had seen two boys and a girl. She even tried showing photos of them. She had some on her phone from breakfast that morning, but Tony, Parvati and Moin were looking at something under the table in all of them, so their faces were not visible.

'Wonder what they were looking at,' she muttered, and walked right into a cart selling fruits. Three oranges fell down and got squished.

'Oye! Look where you're going!' shouted the fruit seller. He was in a foul mood because someone had stolen a whole bunch of bananas from his cart earlier that morning. It was hard enough keeping the monkeys away, without having to deal with thieving humans.

'Enough is enough,' he yelled. 'First, they steal my bananas, now you squish my oranges! How is a man to make a living in this town?' He wheeled his cart away, fuming and muttering about going back to his village.

Mrs Kapuur called out an apology and turned away, not realizing that the only clue to the children's whereabouts had just walked off in a huff.

She saw an old man sitting on a bench, watching people on the road. 'Did you see a girl and two boys walking this way, sir?' she asked him.

'No, but I saw a very suspicious-looking parrot,' he said seriously. 'Was it yours?'

Mrs Kapuur left in a hurry. Getting into a conversation about a dodgy parrot was definitely not going to help her find the children.

She went into a shop which sold all kinds of random things—balloons, caps, wigs, false moustaches, chocolates, fridge magnets, cheese, notebooks, goli soda. She remembered that many of the children had spent a lot of time in the shop.

'Did you see a girl and two boys in blue-and-yellow uniforms?'

The man in the shop wore thick glasses, which made his eyes look like bulbs. His hair, which was usually gelled and combed down, was standing up on end.

'Blue and yellow?' he asked. 'Are you a teacher from that school with blue-and-yellow uniforms?'

'Yes!' Mrs Kapuur cried, quite sure that she'd finally found someone who could give her a clue to the whereabouts of the missing children.

'Good. You owe me six hundred and seventy-seven rupees,' he said, pulling out a notebook with a lot of numbers written in it. 'Those children came here and turned this place upside down! And then some of them went off without paying. Here is the list.'

Mrs Kapuur paid the man, took the list and left, after making sure that the children who had left without paying were not the children she was looking for.

She did one more round of the mall road, asking everyone she saw if they had seen the three children.

No one had seen them. Or if they'd seen them, they hadn't noticed them. Or if they had noticed them, they didn't remember them.

Finally, Mrs Kapuur sat down on a bench and, with trembling hands, took out her phone to make some calls.

MONKEY ROCK

Kooki screamed. Just when he thought he was recovering, he had seen the pink creature again.

It all began when five parents, one principal and one principal's wife landed at the hill station. They first went to the police station and met the sub-inspector, whose name was Rajendra Rajan.

Sub-inspector Rajan said, 'Arrey, children will be children. They are like monkeys, no. Must have gone off somewhere to eat ice cream. Or maybe bananas. Hahaha! Just like monkeys!'

Mrs Kaif had a strong urge to biff him on the nose. She took a deep breath and remembered her t'ai chi master.

Mrs Kooki did not have a t'ai chi master, so she had no such qualms. She didn't biff the policeman, but she went up to him and poked a finger in his chest.

'You listen to me!' she said, staring into his eyes. The burly man began to shake. 'Those are small children. If anything happens to them, I will personally make sure you never sit on that seat ever again.'

It wasn't clear to SI Rajan whether she was threatening to spank him or report him, but both options made his blood run cold, so he quickly said, 'Madam, madam, we will do our very best, madam.'

'Anh,' said Kooki, who had been quietly admiring his wife's tactics. 'Better to do your best always, no?'

'Hawaldar!' shouted SI Rajan.

Hawaldar Jeevan Kumar ran into the room. When he saw Mrs Kooki, he stopped with a hunted look in his eyes.

After he had run into the little lady waving her umbrella at a mob, he had told himself that he needed to get away from the city. Being a policeman in the city was too stressful. He asked for a transfer for health reasons, so they sent him to a hill station.

It would be quiet, they said. It would be crowded, but the people were much more

laid back, they said. Nothing ever happens there, except for the occasional tourist losing a cell phone, they said.

He'd agreed, because any place where little ladies did not ride scooters like maniacs and brandish umbrellas at mobs seemed like a good place to be. But here she was again.

Was she following him? Or was she a figment of his imagination, that turned up everywhere to torment him? Did he need to see a psychiatrist?

But one look at his terrified boss, and he knew he was not imagining her. She was definitely here. JK's Adam's apple bobbed up and down in shock.

When Mrs Kooki turned and saw JK, she let out a happy squeak. 'Hello!' she called delightedly. 'It's you! Remember me? It's me!' She brandished an imaginary umbrella and did a little jig.

SI Rajan looked even more terrified. JK looked even more shocked.

Thinking he hadn't yet recognized her, the little lady began to act like she was riding a scooter. 'DRRRRRR. Remember? You stopped me, but then you let me go? DRRRRRR?'

This looked like it could go on forever. The SI seemed to have totally lost his tongue. So the parents stepped in and divided the party up into three groups. They would go to different parts of the town to look for the children.

To JK's secret horror, he was sent with Kooki, Mrs Kooki and one of the boys' mothers, who seemed to be having some sort of attack. Every now and then, she stopped, waved her hands like clouds, took a deep breath and struck a strange pose.

'It helps me calm down,' she said sheepishly when she saw JK look at her in alarm.

JK wished again that he had become a postman, like his father. The life of a policeman was too complicated for him.

'Why?' Parvati asked. 'Why did you have to bring it? And if you brought it, why on earth did you let it have bananas? Why?'

'I've been trying to tell you what happened, but you won't listen to me!' Moin complained. He was tired, he was hungry, and he was fed up of being responsible for a stupid monster that did what it liked.

'I couldn't stop and listen, could I? We had to run after the monster! Tell me now.'

They were in the middle of what looked like a jungle. There were bushes and trees everywhere, and the sound of traffic was muffled and distant. If they screamed, no one would hear them.

The monster was nowhere to be seen, and they couldn't go back without it—even if they managed to find their way out, which seemed more and more unlikely.

The three children sat down on some rocks and caught their breath.

'It was my fault!' Tony said.

'What?' Moin had been cursing himself for being careless.

'It told me that it would tell me three new rules if I let it out of your suitcase. So I did, and instead of telling me, it slipped into your backpack just as we were leaving. It fooled me!' Tony was very, very upset. He was the only one who supported the monster, so to be tricked by it seemed like a terrible betrayal.

'Maybe it will tell you the rules when we get back,' said Parvati. Tony was always so optimistic that it was a bit alarming to see him looking sad.

'If we ever get back,' Moin said.

Moin was always pessimistic, so it didn't alarm Parvati very much. It irritated her, though.

'Of course we'll get back,' she said. 'As soon as we find that stupid monster!'

'Did you notice something?' asked Tony suddenly. 'There are no monkeys!'

'That's true!' exclaimed Moin.

While they were chasing the monster, the trees had been full of chattering, nattering monkeys. But now, there was not a single monkey around.

'Do you think they'll kill the monster?' asked Moin, anxious.

'I don't think monsters can die,' said Tony.

As they sat quietly thinking about this, they heard something. It was too faint to make out the words or the tune, but that voice was unmistakable even when it was so far away.

The three of them ran towards it.

Suddenly, they came to a clearing which seemed to have monkeys on every inch of its surface—on the trees, on the ground, and some even on top of each other.

In the middle, on a large rock, stood the monster. At its feet was the huge bunch of bananas that it had stolen from the fruit seller, which the monkeys had then run away with. It seemed to have got them back.

The monster looked happy, and it was singing. And a group of monkeys standing around it sang what sounded like a chorus.

*There's only one fruit
For me and you.
What's that?*

Monkeys: *Chitter chatter chitter chatter chit chit chat!*

*It tastes like sugar
And feels like goo.
What's that?*

('Bananas!' said Tony.)

Monkeys: *Chitter chatter chitter chatter chit chit chat!*

*It's squishy as mush
And sticky as glue.
What's that?*

('It likes overripe bananas,' nodded Moin.)

Monkeys: *Chitter chatter chitter chatter chit chit chat!*

*It's starts with a B
And ends with a U.
What's that?*

('That's just bad spelling,' muttered Parvati.)

Monkeys: *Chitter chatter chitter chatter chit chit chat!*

As the monster sang, the monkeys tittered and nattered and danced. It would have been quite a delightful sight if the song hadn't been so bad. And the song and dance would have gone on and on and on, if the monster hadn't suddenly decided to start throwing bananas at its audience.

After that there was complete chaos.

The monster kept singing, though now the song had changed:

A bish! A bosh!
Banana squash!

A shosh! A shish!
Banana squish!

A burp! A belch!
Banana squelch!

A chick! A chock!
Banana squawk!

A daze! A dream!
Banana—

Someone screamed.

So loudly that all the monkeys disappeared.

Moin ran up to the rock, the monster flattened itself and hopped into his pocket, and by the time Mrs Kooki and Mrs Kaif reached the clearing, there was nothing to be seen except the children.

Kooki, who had reached the clearing half a minute before the others, stood where he was, mouth open in shock, and pointed with a trembling finger at the rock.

'Pink thing,' he squeaked. 'Look!'

But there was nothing on the rock but some squished bananas.

TAIL END

'I want to grow a tail,' said the monster.

'Gah!' said Moin. 'This is what I've been listening to every day for the past week!'

Moin, Parvati and Tony had been grounded for a week after the hill-station fiasco. Parvati had spent the time practising on her violin, and Tony had caught up with his reading. He especially read up on time travel, because he was still stuck on the theory that the monster was a time traveller.

'Do you have a wife?' he asked the monster now. He had come upon a book called *The Time Traveler's Wife*, and though he had no idea what it was about, he felt he needed to get that out of the way.

'Yuck! Monsters don't get married,' said the monster. Tony heaved a sigh of relief. The idea of the monster having a wife had made him a little anxious.

'Is that a rule?' he asked eagerly.

'Nope,' said the monster. 'It's not even a rule because no one ever thought of it. Like there's no rule about a tail because no one thought of it. If they had, I'm sure they would have made it a rule for all monsters to have tails. Tails are so awesome!'

Ever since meeting the monkeys, the monster had been going on about wanting a tail. So while Parvati played the violin and Tony researched time travel, Moin had had to listen to the monster moaning on and on about a tail.

'At least it didn't start singing about it,' Parvati consoled Moin.

'I did make up a song!' the monster replied, standing up on the table. 'I was waiting for an audience. It's boring to sing to only one person. It's one of my best. Listen!'

If I had a tail, I could
Swing, swing, swing it.
Over the trees I could
Wing, wing, wing it.

So get me a tail!
A long and zinging tail!

Go find a tail and
Bring, bring, bring it.

If I had a tail, I could
Throw, throw, throw it.
All through the day I could
Show, show, show it.
So get me a tail!
A long and flowing tail!
Get me a tail and I'll
Grow, grow, grow it.

If I had a tail, I could—

'Uff! Stop!' said Parvati, covering her ears with a pillow. 'Do you have to sing so loudly? And can't you make a little sense?'

Tony was frowning thoughtfully. 'Can you add a tail now? And will it grow? Your hair grew because you put that oil, but what would make a tail grow?'

'Please, please, please don't give it any ideas now,' begged Moin. He lived in constant fear of what trouble the monster would get him into next. 'I'll tell you what. I'll make a tail with a piece of paper, and we can stick it on.'

'We can use a streamer,' said Parvati. 'You have any? Would you like a nice, colourful tail?' she asked the monster.

But when the monster saw the streamer, it was very upset. 'It's too thin! I can't hang upside down with this! It'll tear, and I'll land on my head.'

'Then maybe you'll get some sense,' Moin muttered. 'Okay, what about cardboard, then?'

'I can't swing with it. It's too stiff.'

'Cloth?' suggested Tony.

Moin pulled out an old tie and said, 'Here. This is a perfect tail.'

'But how do we put it on?' asked Parvati. 'Should we pin it on?'

'What!? You can't stick a pin into me!' yelled the monster.

'Okay, okay,' said Moin. 'Let me think. What about sticking it with glue?'

So they tried that. But the glue would not stick on the monster.

'You should have drawn a tail when you drew me,' sulked the monster.

'You described yourself, didn't you? You should have described a tail, then. I couldn't draw something you didn't describe, could I?'

'You draw so badly anyway that if I'd asked you to draw a tail, you would have drawn an earthworm. What use would that have been? I want a tail that I can swing with.'

'Then you should have gone and hidden under Picasso's bed, I told you. Or under

some other artist's bed. Why me? Why, why, why?' Moin scowled and turned his back on the monster.

There was silence, while Moin, Parvati and Tony sat and thought of all the crazy things that had happened because the monster had turned up under Moin's bed and asked him to draw it.

'WAIT!' yelled Tony. 'I've had the most brilliant idea! Why don't you draw a tail on the first drawing you drew? The one which made it appear! That might work.'

'Can we do that?' asked Moin. But the monster had gone off into the cupboard to sulk and had fallen asleep.

MONSTER RULE 320

Human products may not have any effect on monsters. (Also see rule number 321.)

'Good idea! Let's try it,' said Parvati.

But there was a problem. Moin had no idea where he had kept that paper. He had torn it off a calendar. But then what had he done with it?

'Do you think your mum has thrown it away?'

'No, she keeps everything I draw,' said Moin sheepishly.

Parvati looked astonished. She couldn't understand why anyone would want to keep a drawing done by Moin.

'Mothers can be blind, I guess,' Tony said wisely.

'So we should ask her,' said Parvati. 'Maybe she's kept it in a portfolio, in case you turn into a famous artist and your paintings become super expensive.' Then she collapsed into a heap because the thought of Moin becoming a famous artist made her cackle helplessly.

'It's not so funny,' muttered Moin.

'It is, just a little bit,' giggled Tony.

The fact was that Moin's mother did keep all his drawings together. She had no hope of him becoming a famous artist, but as she told Mr Kaif, 'I don't want him to think we don't value his work.' Mr Kaif objected to calling Moin's drawings 'work' because it implied that there was some skill or effort involved. But he sensibly said nothing.

Moin turned his mother's study upside down till he found the folder—and sure enough, the drawing of the monster was in it.

When he got to his room, the monster was awake and looking very harassed.

'I told you I can't remember them,' it said.

After the monkey fiasco, Tony had asked the monster to keep its word about telling him three rules. The monster had only been able to remember rule number 71.

MONSTER RULE 71

A monster can leave the human world under some circumstances. (Also see rule numbers 228 and 364.)

Parvati had got very excited when she heard this. 'That means it can go!'

'But it's no good, unless it remembers rules 228 and 364,' Moin had moaned.

So now, Parvati was prompting it to remember what rules 228 and 364 were, and the monster was getting very irritated.

Tony tried to mollify the monster. 'Look, we're trying to get you a tail,' he said. 'Moin has brought the drawing he made when you described yourself. He is going to add a tail to it.'

Moin put the drawing down and picked up a pink crayon.

'I don't want a pink tail!' yelled the monster. 'Make it blue.'

Moin took the crayon and drew a long blue tail on the pink monster. He sat back and beamed. He was quite proud of the tail. It was long and, well, blue. *But it looked very nice*, he thought.

Parvati shook her head sadly. Tony looked at the monster carefully to see if a blue tail was beginning to appear.

'Hold it up!' he said to Moin.

The monster stood in front of the drawing. But it remained tailless.

It turned around and jiggled its bottom at the drawing. But nothing happened.

Parvati peered at the drawing. 'Your tail is not touching the monster's bottom,' she told Moin. 'No wonder nothing is happening.'

She took the first crayon she could find—which happened to be pink—and filled in the gap between the tail and the monster's body in the drawing. Then she thought it looked weird, so she decided to make a polka-dotted design on the blue tail.

'Now look!' she said, and held out the drawing, but still, nothing happened.

The monster was inconsolable. It started to sing in a wailing, howling voice.

Oh for a tail,
A tail, a tail!
Such a simple thing to aaaask.

Just a loooong
And wiiiinding tail
It's not a haaaard taaaaask.

Oh, oh, oh
I waaaant a tail—

'Maybe it has to be Moin,' Tony suddenly shouted, partly because he had a brilliant thought and partly to stop the monster from singing.

'What do you mean?' asked Parvati.

Moin had stuffed his ears with cotton and closed his eyes, so Tony had to shake him and say, '*You* hold up the drawing!'

So Moin did, and the monster's tail appeared—pink and blue and polka-dotted, it was a horrible sight, and Parvati wished she'd never done it.

But it was too late. The monster got a long, winding, pink-and-blue tail. It swung off the fan and whooped in delight.

I can sing sing sing!
I can dance dance dance!
I can swing swing swing!
I can prance prance prance!
I can play play play—
With the breeze breeze breeze!
I can sway sway sway—
In the trees trees trees!

It wouldn't stop. Downstairs, Mr and Mrs Kaif ordered another pack of cotton for their ears.

'Now I have a monkey monster. Thanks a lot,' said Moin bitterly to Tony and Parvati.

But they had fled.

Anushka Ravishankar is a children's writer based in Chennai. She has written over forty books for children, some of which have won international awards. Her books include the Smartypants series, *Elephants Never Forget*, *Rooster for a Pet* and *Ogd*. Several of her books have been translated into Dutch, German, Italian, Spanish and other languages.

Anitha Balachandran lives in Bangalore. She is an animation filmmaker, researcher and illustrator who enjoys telling stories and creating images by hand.